CULTURE IN ACTION

Art That Moves

Animation Around the World

John Bliss

Chicago, Illinois

www.heinemannraintree.com
Visit our website to find out more information about Heinemann-Raintree books.

To order:
☎ Phone 888-454-2279
🖳 Visit www.heinemannraintree.com to browse our catalog and order online.

©2011 Raintree
an imprint of Capstone Global Library, LLC
Chicago, Illinois

Edited by Louise Galpine, Megan Cotugno, and Abby Colich
Designed by Ryan Frieson
Original illustrations © Capstone Global Library, Ltd.
Illustrated by Cavedweller Studio, Randy Schirz
Picture research by Liz Alexander
Originated by Capstone Global Library, Ltd.
Printed and bound in China by China Translation & Printing Services, Ltd.

14 13 12 11 10
10 9 8 7 6 5 4 3 2 1

Library of Congress Cataloging-in-Publication Data
Bliss, John.
 Art that moves : animation around the world / John Bliss.
-- 1st ed.
    p. cm. -- (Culture in action)
 Includes bibliographical references and index.
 ISBN 978-1-4109-3922-7 (hc)
 1. Animated films--Juvenile literature. I. Title. II. Title:
Animation around the world.
 NC1765.B58 2011
 791.43'34--dc22
                    2009051125

Acknowledgments

The author and publishers are grateful to the following for permission to reproduce copyright material:

We would like to thank the following for permission to reproduce photographs: Alamy pp. 6 (© Robert Harding Picture Library Ltd), 8 (© Mary Evans Picture Library); Corbis pp. 12 (© Louis Quail), 20 (© Bettmann), 22 (© Daniel Deme/epa); Getty Images p. 7 (Science & Society Picture Library); iStockphoto p. 16 (© dem10); Rex Features pp. 4, 19 (© 20thC. Fox/Everett), 10 (Everett Collection), 14 (Stewart Cook), 15, 21 (© W.Disney/Everett), 17 (© Warner Br/Everett), 18 (© Everett Collection), 25 (© Sony/Everett), 27 (© Focus Features/Everett); The Kobal Collection pp. 5 (WARNER BROS), 24 (TVC), 26 (Walt Disney Pictures/Walden Media).

Cover photograph of Brambly Hedge TV animation reproduced with permission of Rex Features (Caroline Mardon).

We would like to thank Jackie Murphy and Susie Hodge for their invaluable help in the preparation of this book.

Every effort has been made to contact copyright holders of any material reproduced in this book. Any omissions will be rectified in subsequent printings if notice is given to the publisher.

All the Internet addresses (URLs) given in this book were valid at the time of going to press. However, due to the dynamic nature of the Internet, some addresses may have changed, or sites may have changed or ceased to exist since publication. While the author and Publishers regret any inconvenience this may cause readers, no responsibility for any such changes can be accepted by either the author or the Publishers.

Author
John Bliss is a writer and teacher who teaches courses in theater and communications.

Literacy consultant
Jackie Murphy is Director of Arts at the Center of Teaching and Learning, Northeastern Illinois University. She works with teachers, artists, and school leaders internationally.

Expert
Susie Hodge is an author and artist with nearly 60 books in print. She has an MA in the History of Art from the University of London and is a Fellow of the Royal Society of Arts. She teaches and lectures on practical art and art and design history to students of all ages.

Contents

Some words are printed in bold, **like this**. You can find out what they mean by looking in the glossary on page 30.

A World of Animation

What is your favorite movie? If you said *WALL-E* (2008), *Chicken Run* (2000), or *Ice Age* (2002), you chose an animated movie. Both kids and adults love animated movies. In 2008 the animated movie *Kung Fu Panda* made more than $600 million in theaters around the world.

Some animated characters are so famous that people recognize them instantly.

Animation around the world

Many countries make animated movies and TV shows. Important animated movies have been made in France and Israel. In Russia and India, animation is a growing art form. Later in this book, you will read about animation from Japan.

Where the Wild Things Are (2009) combines live action and animation. Other effects are created by special costumes and animatronics, which are robotic puppets.

Animation is everywhere

Animation is used in movies, television shows, and commercials. Even **live-action** movies (movies with human actors) sometimes include animated characters or **special effects** that use animation. All video games are made using computer animation. It is hard to go through a day without seeing some kind of animation.

Constantly changing

Early cartoons were drawn completely by hand. Today most animation is done with computers. Artists are using new tools to create new kinds of animated characters. Who knows what the future will bring?

What does it mean?

The word *animation* comes from the Latin word *anima*, which means "life." In an animated movie or television show, still pictures seem to come to life!

Early Attempts at Animation

For as long as people have been making art, they have been trying to make art move. Ancient cave drawings show animals with extra legs or heads. The artists put the animals' legs in more than one position in order to show that they were running.

A Persian bowl from 5,200 years ago has a **sequence** (series) of paintings that show a goat eating from a tree. Greek sculptures from 450 BCE show people in a series of poses, as if they are moving.

This mural is from an ancient Egyptian tomb. The sequence of pictures looks like **frames** (individual pictures) from an animated movie.

Making pictures move

In the 1800s, people started making machines that would make pictures appear to move. One of the first was the **zoetrope**, invented in 1834. The zoetrope is like a drum, with pictures on the inside and slits cut into the side. As you spin the drum and look through the slits, the pictures seem to move.

In 1868 an English printer made the first **flip book**. He bound a series of pictures together in a small book. Flipping the pages made the pictures seem to move.

A modern zoetrope

Academy Award—winning movie director Francis Ford Coppola received a zoetrope as a gift from a friend. He liked it so much that he named his **studio** American Zoetrope. A studio is a company that makes movies.

The pictures around the edge of this disk seem to move when they are viewed one after another. This image could be projected like a movie.

Eadweard Muybridge

Eadweard (pronounced "Edward") Muybridge was an English photographer who worked in the 1800s. By using many cameras that took pictures one after another, he was able to capture the movement of people and animals. At the time, nobody knew how animals really moved. Most artists showed animals running with their legs sticking out like rocking horses.

Later, Muybridge put his pictures together to re-create the motion he photographed. Some of his techniques are still used to create **special effects** in movies today.

In 1872 Leland Stanford of California said that when a horse ran, all four feet left the ground at the same time. Muybridge took these photographs to prove that he was right.

Make a flip book

A flip book is simple to make. All you need is a pencil, some paper, and a little imagination.

Steps to follow:

1. Decide what you want to animate. You might try a volcano erupting or a flower opening. Even if you do not think you can draw well, you can make a stick figure move. Keep it simple!

2. Before you start making your flip book, sketch out some ideas.

3. Staple at least 10 small sheets of paper together into a pad. Draw your first picture on the last page, close to the outside edge. Starting with the last page and working forward will make it easy to line up your drawings.

4. On the next page, draw another picture. It should be the same as the first picture, with a small change. Flip between the two pictures to compare them as you work.

5. Draw more pictures in the series. Remember the change between each drawing should be slow. Flip through the pages to see the final animation.

Once you are happy with your book, add a title page and then show others!

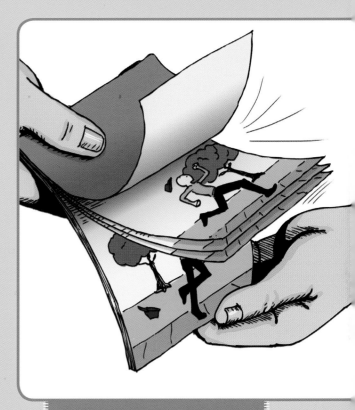

Flipping through your drawings makes the pictures seem to move. You can flip the pages in the other direction to make the animation move in reverse.

How Does Animation Work?

Animation depends on an optical illusion, or trick of the eye. What we see as a moving picture is really a series of still pictures. When we see the pictures quickly, one after another, our brain puts them together into a moving picture.

Drawn by hand

Early animated movies were drawn completely by hand. Artists drew every **frame** that was used in the movie. They had to make sure that each picture was exactly alike. In some of these old cartoons, the background wiggles because the drawings are not perfectly matched.

Winsor McCay made *Gertie the Dinosaur* in 1914. Gertie is considered the first real cartoon character.

Cels to the rescue

In 1914 a new **process** called "**cel** animation" was invented. With this process, the background remains the same. Animators only have to redraw the part of the picture that is moving. They draw this on a transparent (see-through) sheet made of **celluloid**, a kind of plastic made from plants. The word *celluloid* was shortened to *cel*, and these sheets became known as "cels." Using cels makes the animator's job much easier.

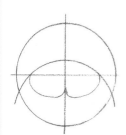 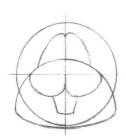  

Creating a cartoon character

The secret to creating many cartoon characters is to use simple shapes, such as circles and ovals. This is true for characters from Mickey Mouse to Homer Simpson. For the character drawn here, the head and eyes are circles.

Other kinds of animation

Cel animation is only one kind of animation. Animators also use clay models, puppets, and even cut-out pieces of paper to make their movies.

Stop-motion animation

In **stop-motion** animation, real objects are filmed one frame at a time. Between each frame, the animator moves the objects a very little bit. When the frames are viewed one after another, the objects seem to move.

Stop motion takes time

Animators making a Wallace and Gromit movie (see page 22) use stop-motion animation. They shoot about 30 frames of film in a day. That is a little more than one second of time in the final movie! Every second of every Wallace and Gromit movie includes 10 to 24 frames.

A Wallace and Gromit animator moves the characters in order to shoot a new frame.

Make it move!

You can make a simple stop-motion movie using a **digital** camera, which uses a computer disk instead of film.

Steps to follow:

1. Ask a friend to be the "model" in your movie.

2. Place your camera on a stable surface, such as a tabletop. Have your friend pose while you take his or her picture.

3. Tell you friend if he should look happy, sad, surprised, or scared. Now have your friend change his or her position slightly while you take another picture. Repeat this process as many times as you like. You can scroll between photos to check the movement.

4. You can add **special effects** to your movie. For example, if you give your friend an object between photos, it will seem to appear in his or her hand out of thin air!

Ask an adult to help input your photos into a movie-making or slideshow program on a computer. Then you can show your movie to other people. Get together with friends and have a film festival!

This drawing shows how four different poses can look like one movement.

Modern Technology

Most animation today is done on computers. Instead of shooting **cels** and backgrounds, drawings are put together **digitally**.

Computer-assisted animation

One kind of digital animation is called computer-assisted animation. This is when the original drawings are still done by hand, but computers are also used to assist, or help out. Animations produced this way can still look as though they were made with traditional cel animation.

Computer animation

Some animation today is created completely on a computer. Animators use special computer programs to create objects and characters and make them move. Moving images on a computer screen, video games, and animated movies all use computer animation.

Video games combine more than one kind of animation. Animators need to create whole worlds, or environments, for characters to move through. Game designers might use one kind of animation for characters and another for the environment.

Video games are interactive, meaning they respond to choices players make. Video game animators have to consider every choice players might make.

CGI

CGI stands for "**computer-generated imagery**." Characters and backgrounds in CGI movies have a **three-dimensional** (**3D**) shape, meaning they have height, width, and depth. Instead of looking flat, as in a traditional hand-drawn animation, CGI characters look more realistic. The characters in *Ratatouille* (2007) and *Flushed Away* (2006) are CGI. In contrast, Mickey Mouse is a traditional, flat animated character.

Most recent animated movies such as *Up* (2009) use CGI. CGI is also used to create **special effects** in **live-action** films.

Toy Story

Toy Story (1995) was the first full-length movie that was animated completely by using CGI.

These characters and backgrounds in the CGI movie *Up* appear more "real" than those in traditional animation.

Models and wire frames

But how does CGI work? CGI is a lot like **stop-motion** animation. But instead of photographing actual objects, animators create models in the computer. They then make these models move.

Objects are created using wire frames. Imagine wrapping a window screen or a piece of netting around an object such as a book or a cup. That is what a wire frame is like. Once a wire frame has been created, the animator can look at the object on his or her computer screen from any angle.

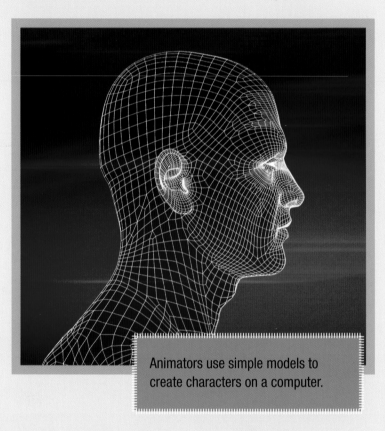

Animators use simple models to create characters on a computer.

Characters are harder to animate, because they move in many different directions at once. Animators create a model of the skeleton of the character, as well as the surface. One character may have hundreds of different "joints" that control his or her movement.

Motion capture

Motion capture is a new way of animating characters. In motion capture, human actors wear many small electronic discs, called **sensors**, on their face and body. The sensors tell the computer where the actor is at all times. The computer tracks the sensors to record the actor's movement. This information is then used to create realistic movement for an animated character.

Award-winning motion capture

Happy Feet (2006), *Monster House* (2006), and *Cars* (2006) were all nominated for Academy Awards in 2007. *Cars* was the only one of the movies that did not use motion- capture technology.

The dance scenes in *Happy Feet* were acted out by real people. Animators used motion-capture technology to record their moves.

Anime

Anime is a Japanese style of animation. Anime characters often have very large facial features that show lots of emotion. Many of the stories are very dramatic. Anime includes traditional animation and computer animation. It has been popular in Japan for many years, but it has only recently spread to other countries.

Manga

Japanese animation started with popular comic books called **manga**. People of all ages read manga, and they are about many subjects. In addition to action and adventure, manga tell stories of romance, mystery, and even history. Some manga characters were developed into anime. For example, the character Astro Boy started as a manga character before he appeared in movies.

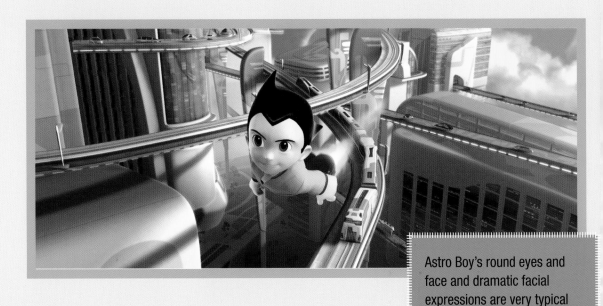

Astro Boy's round eyes and face and dramatic facial expressions are very typical of anime.

Anime takes off

Anime did not get noticed outside Japan until the 1970s. During this period, the success of *Star Wars* (1977) in Western countries made audiences want more science fiction stories. Many anime told stories of giant robots and outer space battles. These movies were then reworked for release in other countries.

Akira, made in 1988, is about a young boy with special powers. It was the first anime to find success outside Japan. The popularity of *Akira* made people look for anime on videocassette. Later, DVDs made older titles available to even more people. Today, anime is more popular than ever.

Akira was the first Japanese animated movie to be successful around the world. It was even more popular in other countries than in Japan.

Pokémon

Pokémon began as a video game. Since then, its characters have been seen in manga, movies, and television shows. The name *Pokémon* is short for "pocket monsters."

Masters of Animation

Many artists have worked in animation. Some artists have changed the way people see and make animation.

Walt Disney

Walt Disney is the most famous animator in the United States, and maybe the world. He was responsible for many important achievements in animation.

Disney made *Steamboat Willie*, the first cartoon with **synchronized** sound, in 1928. Disney continued to experiment with sound in a series of musical **shorts** (movie longer than 30 minutes) called *Silly Symphonies* (1929 to 1939). In 1937 he made *Snow White and the Seven Dwarfs*, the first **feature**-length (longer than an hour) animated film. He continued to shape how people made animated movies until his death in 1966.

And the Oscar goes to . . .

Walt Disney (1901–1966) was nominated for 59 Academy Awards and won 22 times. Most of these awards were for shorts. *Beauty and the Beast* (1991), made by Disney **Studios**, is the only feature-length animated film ever to be nominated for a Best Picture Academy Award.

Walt Disney started making animations when he was still in his twenties.

Hayao Miyazaki

Hayao Miyazaki is the most well-known Japanese animator in the world. But before 1997 he was mostly unknown outside of Japan.

Miyazaki's film *Nausicaä of the Valley of the Wind* (1984) was the first movie he both wrote alone and directed. The success of *Nausicaä* made **anime** more respected by many people.

Since *Nausicaä*, Miyazaki has created many popular anime. *Princess Mononoke* (1997) won Best Picture at the Japanese Academy Awards in 1998. *Spirited Away* (2001) and *Howl's Moving Castle* (2004) are the most successful animated movies ever made in Japan.

Spirited Away is the most successful movie—animated or otherwise—ever released in Japan.

Nick Park

Nick Park is best known for his characters Wallace and Gromit, whom he introduced in the animated short *A Grand Day Out* in 1989. The same year, he made *Creature Comforts*. The two animations competed against each other for both an Academy Award and a British Academy of Film and Television Arts (BAFTA) Award. *A Grand Day Out* won the BAFTA for Best Animated Short Film, while *Creature Comforts* won the Academy Award for Best Animated Short.

Nick Park is shown here with his BAFTA award.

Animated voices

Voice actors help bring characters to life and give them their personality. Peter Sallis, the voice of Wallace, has acted on stage and in movies for more than 50 years. He is known for his role as Clegg in the long-running UK television series *Last of the Summer Wine* (begun 1973). Today, many Hollywood stars want to work on animated movies.

Make your own soundtrack

Pictures are only part of what makes cartoons fun. Voices, music, and sound effects are also important parts. They can make us laugh, jump, or even cry.

Steps to follow:

1. Experiment with musical instruments to find sounds you might use in a cartoon. Slide whistles, cymbals, and harmonicas are popular instruments.

2. Find and create things around the house that you can use to make music. For example, you can hit on a pot with a spoon or rattle coins in a jar.

3. Play a cartoon with the sound off. Watch for places where adding sounds would make the cartoon more fun. Look for movement of characters and objects, changes in facial expression, or major actions.

4. Use your instruments to create new sounds for the background and **special effects**. Experiment and have fun!

Get together with friends and create a new sound track for a cartoon. Perform your work for your class.

Experiment using your instruments to create different moods for a cartoon. Practice makes perfect!

23

Not Just for Kids

Animation is not just for children. Many cartoons from the 1930s and 1940s were made to play in movie theaters before the **feature**-length movies were shown.

Animation on television

Animated programs have been a part of television for many years. In the 1960s, *The Flintstones* (1960–1966), *The Bugs Bunny Show* (1960–1975), and many other animated shows aired during evening hours, when adults watched.

In the past 20 years, there has been an explosion of animation on television. Some shows, such as *The Simpsons* (begun 1989), include humor that both adults and kids can enjoy. Others, such as *Family Guy* (begun 1999), are meant for adults.

¡Ay, caramba!

The Simpsons has aired on U.S. television since 1989. There have been games, books, and a movie based on the series. In 2010 the show aired its 450th episode.

The television special *The Snowman* was first shown in 1982. It became so popular that it now airs every year in some countries.

Movies for adults

In recent years, animated movies with plots and ideas that are meant for adults have become popular. *Persepolis* (2007) is about a young girl growing up during the 1979 revolution in Iran. *Waltz With Bashir* (2008) is about war in the Middle East. Many of these films have won important awards.

The movie *Persepolis* is based on a graphic novel by the same name. A graphic novel tells its story with pictures and words, like a comic book.

New Trends in Animation

Computer animation is still very new. The exciting **special effects** we see today may seem like hand-drawn pictures in 10 years. As long as there are new artists and new technologies, there will be new forms of animation.

Realistic characters

Some animators want their characters to look more real, rather than like hand-drawn creations. For example, directors used **motion-capture** technology to create lifelike animated characters in *The Polar Express* (2004) and the *Lord of the Rings* trilogy (2001–2003).

Animators are working on new ways to make hair and clothing move in realistic ways. In 2008 a computer animation company revealed a video of "Emily," a **CGI** woman who looks just like a real person.

Animators working on the Lion character Aslan in *The Chronicles of Narnia: The Lion, The Witch, and the Wardrobe* (2005) shot video of actual lions to be sure Aslan's movement was accurate.

Three-dimentional

Animators are experimenting with new ways to create **three-dimensional**, or **3D**, effects. CGI characters and backgrounds look three-dimensional, rather than flat. New technology makes the action seem to come off the screen. *Monsters vs. Aliens* (2009) and *Coraline* (2009) are two recent 3D movies. Dreamworks, the **studio** that produced *Monsters vs. Aliens*, plans to make all its animated movies 3D from now on. Who knows what other changes will happen in years to come?

Forward into the past

A new **process** in CGI is called "**cel**-shaded animation." This is a way to make images created on a computer look as though they were drawn by hand.

Coraline is one of the latest 3D animated movies. These movies require special projectors (machines that show moving images) and glasses to view their effects.

Timeline

C. 30,000 BCE	Cave paintings in France show animals with multiple heads and legs.
C. 2300 BCE	Egyptian tombs are decorated with scenes from daily life.
180 CE	An early version of the **zoetrope** is created in China.
1834	British mathematician William George Horner creates the first modern zoetrope.
1855	British inventor Alexander Parkes invents **celluloid**.
1868	British printer John Barnes Linnet **patents** (claims as his own invention) the Kineograph, also known as the **flip book**.
1878	British photographer Eadweard Muybridge photographs a running horse using a series of 24 cameras.
1892	French scientist Charles-Émile Reynaud creates the first animated pictures, which are drawn on long strips of paper.
1906	U.S. filmmaker J. Stuart Blackton makes the first animated film, called *Humorous Phases of Funny Faces*.
1911	U.S. animator Winsor McCay makes a **short** cartoon starring his comic strip character Little Nemo.
1914	U.S. filmmakers John R. Bray and Earl Hurd seek to patent a **process** that simplifies animation production. They paint the backgrounds of animated movies on celluloid.
1917	*Imokawa Mukuzo, The Janitor*, the first Japanese animated film, is released.
1923	U.S. animator Walt Disney and his brother Roy found Disney Brothers Cartoon **Studio**.

1925	U.S. animator Willis O'Brien uses **stop-motion** animation to bring dinosaurs to life in *The Lost World*.
1927	Warner Brothers releases *The Jazz Singer*, the first "talking picture," meaning characters speak some words. In the past, the only sound in movies had been background music.
1928	Walt Disney makes *Steamboat Willie*, the first **synchronized** sound cartoon.
1932	Walt Disney's *Flowers and Trees* wins the first Academy Award for Animated Short Film.
1933	U.S. animator Ub Iwerks creates a camera that films several layers of **cels** at the same time. This gives the final movie a **three-dimensional** look.
1954	*Animal Farm* becomes the first British animated **feature-** length movie released worldwide.
1973	*Westworld* is the first movie to use **CGI**.
1987	Pixar's short film *Luxo Jr.* is the first CGI animation nominated for an Academy Award.
1992	Disney's *Beauty and the Beast* is the first animated film nominated for the Academy Award for Best Picture.
1993	In *Jurassic Park*, realistic-looking CGI dinosaurs appear in scenes with human actors.
1995	*Toy Story* is the first feature-length CGI feature film.
2006	Disney buys the Pixar animation studio.

Glossary

anime Japanese style of animation

cel short for "celluloid," it is a transparent sheet used in animation

celluloid bendable plastic made from plant materials. Early movies were shot on celluloid.

computer-generated imagery (CGI) moving pictures created on a computer

digital using information that can be read by a computer

feature movie that is an hour or longer. Movies you see in a theater are all feature length.

flip book book that uses a series of pictures to create animation

frame individual picture in an animation. Movies are projected at 24 frames per second.

live action movie or video that is acted out by living actors, rather than animated characters

manga Japanese comic book

motion capture film making process that records the movement of human actors to create animated characters

patent to claim ownership of an invention

process series of steps in making a product

sensor electronic device that sends and receives signals

sequence several things following one after another

short live action or animated movie that is shorter than 30 minutes

special effect filmmaking trick that makes imaginary events seem real

stop motion type of animation in which real objects are filmed one frame at a time

studio company that makes movies

synchronize to happen at the same time

three-dimensional (3D) appearing to have height, width, and depth. Three-dimensional characters seem round, unlike two-dimensional characters, which seem flat. The term can also refer to an effect in which objects seem to come off the screen into the audience.

zoetrope early animation device. A zoetrope is like a spinning drum, with pictures on the inside that can be viewed through slits.

Find Out More

Books

Hahn, Don. *The Alchemy of Animation: Making an Animated Film in the Modern Age.* New York: Disney, 2008.

Hart, Christopher. *Humongous Book of Cartooning.* New York: Watson-Guptill, 2009.

Miles, Liz. *Culture in Action: Movie Special Effects.* Chicago: Raintree, 2010.

DVDs

Pixar Short Films Collection, vol. 1 (Walt Disney, 2007).
This is a collection of early short films from the Pixar studio, including Luxo Jr.

Winsor McCay: The Master Edition (Milestone, 2004).
This contains early cartoons, from 1911 to 1921, by Winsor McCay.

Websites

Aardman Animations
www.aardman.com
This is the website of Aardman Animations, with links to its characters and shows, as well as a virtual studio tour.

Origins of American Animation
http://memory.loc.gov/ammem/oahtml/oahome.html
This feature contains 21 animated films from 1900 to 1921.

Scratch Program
http://scratch.mit.edu
This is a simple program that helps kids create and share animation on the Internet.

Index